The Gospel According to B.

Poems

by Benjamin Bagocius

Attention schools and businesses: for discounted copies on large orders, please contact the publisher directly.

For information contact:
Unsolicited Press
Portland, Oregon
www.unsolicitedpress.com
orders@unsolicitedpress.com
619-354-8005

Cover Design: Kathryn Gerhardt
Editor: S.R. Stewart

ISBN: 978-1-963115-04-8

For my parents, Paul and Cindy Bagocius

CONTENTS

JERUSALEM

Acknowledgments

A handful of poems, some with slightly different titles and in slightly different versions, appear in the following journals, whose editors I thank:

After the Pause: "Yeshua's Notes While Reading *The Epic of Gilgamesh*," "Yeshua's Friends Wait Outside while He Finishes Reading *Gilgamesh*," "Yeshua Reads the Last Page of *Gilgamesh*. A Friend Tells Him to Hurry Up," and "Yeshua Wonders if He'd Consider Gilgamesh a Messiah."

Offerings: Poems Written during Tiferet Journal's Spiritual Poetry Course, May-July 2020: "Yeshua Chooses Seven Crayons: Learning to Write Cursive" and "Jesus Drafts His Paper for the Teachers Conference."

Hika: "Yeshua Chooses Seven Crayons: Starfish on the Beach."

Soul-Lit: "Why Yeshua Changed Water to Wine," "Mary's Biographer Reflects on Three Ceramic Shoes," "The Podcast Host Asks Jesus to Explain Again Because Listeners Want to Understand," and "Jesus's Parable of the Windy Day."

Tiferet: "Jesus Gives the Keynote Address at the National Speech & Debate Tournament."

Pensive: "Man from Sodom Explain Resurrection."

Untold Volumes: "Salome Listens to Yeshua."

Santa Clara Review: "Jesus Heals a Gay Man."

Our Church Too: "Yeshua Guesses Deuteronomy's Writer Had Never Been Kissed by a Man from Sodom" and "Maybe Deuteronomy's Writer *Had* Been Kissed by a Man from Sodom."

Tomorrow and Tomorrow: "One of the Wise Men Explains Why He Became an Astronomer" and "Yeshua Rereads the *Iliad*'s Final Line. It Speaks to Something Deep Inside Him."

Creative Commitments: "Three Wise Men."

Journal of Feminist Studies in Religion: "Yeshua Sits Cross-Legged with His Classmates and Listens to Artemis's Parable of the Soccer Match."

I thank the following family members, friends, and colleagues for their support and enthusiasm for my work as a writer: My parents Paul and Cindy Bagocius, Katherine Judith Anderson, Deborah Bagocius, Scott Bagocius, Blayne Barnes, Anthony Bates, Mary Anne Burrows, Megan Coder, Carl DuPont, Diana Dunn, Shandu Foster, Mara Inglezakis, Rebecca Kent, Deborah Ann Krishnan, Hill Krishnan, Tanja Kummerfeld,, Eleanor Lambert, Aryakorn Joy Phaphouvaninh, Angelina Rodríguez, and Tera Stubblefield.

Preface: A Queer Gospel in Poetry

Many readers have heard of the four gospels canonized in the New Testament: Matthew, Mark, Luke, and John. But there are hundreds, perhaps thousands, of other gospels, including The Gospel of Truth, of Thomas, of Mary, and of Judas. In writing *The Gospel According to B.*, I join the ancient tradition of gospel writers who never knew, met, saw, heard, shared history with, or spoke the same language as the man about whom they wrote, Yeshua ben Yosef, otherwise known as Jesus of Nazareth.

This poetry collection, like all gospels, understands the imagination as a gateway to the sacred. Canonical New Testament scriptures are extraordinary works of the sacred imagination, since "none of these Christian writings," Episcopal priest and writer John Shelby Spong points out, emerge from a writer's "eyewitness account" of Jesus of Nazareth. The Apostle Paul, perhaps early Christianity's most vocal advocate, "never claimed in any of his letters that he knew the Jesus who lived in history," Spong writes. Having eyewitness accounts of the Jesus "who lived in history," for Spong, is irrelevant to the message that gospel and epistolary writers convey. Important to them, Spong continues, is not to establish consensus about "dates, names, places, and events," about which "there are serious conflicts" across canonical scriptures. Neither is it of highest importance among gospel writers "to contain" with historical accuracy "the words Jesus spoke," since no writing exists of Jesus's actual words in his native Aramaic. Put another way, no New Testament writing "is written in the language" Jesus "spoke." The gospels and epistles are "written in Greek," Spong reminds us, and were translated into Latin and German before finding their way into English variations such as the King James or the New International versions readers of this collection might know today. Yet achieving linguistic accuracy, as Spong sees it, is less important to gospel writers, including myself, than entering the divine imagination Jesus inhabited. Writers of the sacred, Spong suggests, limn "a dimension of timelessness in which a presence" we might "call God ultimately resides." *The Gospel According to B.* elaborates a spirit of wonder, reverence, and imagination about divine presence shared by other gospels, from canonical ones such as Matthew to more obscure ones such as The Gospel of Philip.

The Gospel According to B. joins other gospels and epistles in its imaginative attempt to fill a gap in written accounts of Jesus's life and teachings. In other words, writers write to add another perspective to the story of Jesus and the divine. According to Spong, for instance, Paul's writing emphasizes what he understands as the importance of personal transformation to Jesus's teachings. Mark was the first gospel writer to use Midrash—the Jewish intellectual and sacred tradition of analyzing and interpreting Hebrew scripture—to narrate Jesus's life to fit ancient texts' predictions about the Messiah. Differently from Paul, Mark was interested in Jesus's biography and started the tradition among gospel writers of answering the question: Who exactly was Jesus of Nazareth, how did he become who he was, and why? Matthew adds to Mark's story by overtly bringing politics into his version of Jesus's life. Luke expands the audience for Jesus's biography by describing him through imagery and storylines common to gentiles. John combines ancient archetypes with contemporary imagery to bring forward a God who is hip to both ancient and modern concerns. Each gospel writer's unique personality enabled him or her to see and deliver something new about Jesus and his message.

The Gospel According to B. carries on this tradition of contributing missing parts to existing versions of the divine. The poems in this collection imagine Jesus's early life and coming of age, from infancy to childhood, adolescence, and young adulthood, periods of development curiously absent in canonical gospels. The poems unfold surprisingly queer dimensions to Jesus's sensibility and era in a form—narrative poetry—that restores Jesus's aesthetic orientation to reality. I do not claim that Jesus identified as sexually queer. No one during his times would have identified sexually, whether as straight, gay, bi, queer, or otherwise, since sexuality in ancient Palestine and Israel was not a category of identity as it has become today. Constructing identity around notions of sexuality instead of family, profession, or God would not have made sense to him and his community. Yet the poems bring forward what might be called Jesus's queer sensibility as someone who did not follow a straight and constricted path to what it means to be human, but who instead queered, or detoured, accepted routes to the divine in oneself and others. Jesus's idea of self and family were not heteronormative, constrained to gender roles of mother, father, daughter, and son. Rather, he queered the idea of self and family by shifting their defining contours from gender to soul. We are not merely men and women, but rather vessels of the divine who share celestial DNA with God. In shaking the self and community loose from gender constraints, Jesus's teachings queered conversations about and experiences of the divine. This poetry collection imagines those wide-ranging conversations and experiences.

I write this conversation in poetry because many scholars consider Jesus a narrative poet. According to religious studies scholar Willis Barnstone, Jesus conveyed his experience of divine reality in spoken Aramaic narrative poetry. Jesus is one of the world's greatest poets, Barnstone writes, yet his poetry has gone unrecognized as such. Jesus's "lyricism has not been heard as poetry" for nearly "two millennia," Barnstone finds. Instead, Jesus's "lyrics got locked up in prose translation," because Western "translators did not understand the prosody of his Semitic poems, which is not as in Western literature based on rhyme, meter, or stanzaic form," Barnstone explains, "but on" "extended narration," or "narrative phrase." *The Gospel According to B.* restores a narrative poetics infused with queer awareness to Jesus's voice, a voice shaped by the rich narrative verse tradition of Hebrew Bible prophets before him.

Most poems in this collection use the name "Yeshua" for Jesus to imagine his life and experiences before his name reached Western ears as "Iesous Chrīstós" toward the turn of the second century, 100 A.D. The final section of this collection uses the name "Jesus," since the poems dialogue with ideas about the man after his influence extends beyond Israel and Palestine.

No matter their specific contributions to the story of Jesus's life, all gospel writers' accounts of Jesus slip between what religious studies scholar Mircea Eliade has famously called "the sacred and the profane," between divine transcendence and everyday detritus. Jesus himself, of course, is said to slip between these two worlds, too: both man and God, mortal and immortal, enmeshed in material daily life and loosened from it in eternity. Like canonical gospels, *The Gospel According to B.* places Jesus in everyday situations—eating, walking, reading, communing, even kissing—to unlock mystical experience (or merging with God and eternity) always accessible in the ordinary here-and-now.

As in other gospels, the Yeshua narrated in these pages is neither bound to ancient Israel and Palestine, nor to other historical and geographical contexts. His spirit of irrational peace, nonsensical oneness, and incomprehensible innocence is alive and well across time and space in the Mesopotamian god Anu and King Gilgamesh, in Greek Gods such as Zeus and Artemis, in someone with whom you might work or study, or in your daughter, son, friend, or cousin. You might recognize this spirit in yourself. While reading, you may even feel called—like Matthew, Mark, Luke, John, and all other gospel writers—to write your own gospel.

I, along with other gospel writers whether canonized or not, invite you to continue the story Jesus told of unpopular, nonsensical, and absurd love. The world is waiting to read the Gospel According to You.

Yeshua Realizes He is Miryam

I did not ask for the seed
God planted inside me

I run to the sea in the middle of the night
and shout to the darkness, *Is there anyone like me*

Gusts, spray of brine

I turn to walk home and notice a statue
on the beach that looks like Mom

She faces the sea

Three Wise Men

People call us magicians

Magic? We just change perspectives

Watch us move
from east to west,
from walking to pausing,
from standing to kneeling

before the secret you hide
in a barn

We know you can't believe it

We turn doubt into wonder
by shifting your concentration to a star
Our wand is poetry

You see nothing but darkness?
Look again at the star we just mentioned

If that doesn't do the trick
we open incense
Myrrh is our backup

Clouds of scent circle under your nose

::poof::

The inconceivable life you lay aside
and do not want

:: inhale :: exhale ::

is now the world's savior

One of the Wise Men Explains Why He Became an Astronomer

An artist showed me his drawing
of a star
in the shape of two men kissing

Their entwined lips were streaks of light,
their hair blew backward like wild horse manes
Their eyes looked into each other's
and into mine

That night I scanned the sky,
and I saw it

The kiss that had always been there

Two men sitting inside Anu's chariot,
their kiss showering the night with sparks
as the Lord drove them across the heavens

Yeshua Played with Dolls

Trucks and cars didn't interest me
They had intricate doors and windows
but none inside

Dolls' eyes were frozen open
They absorbed everything

Maybe they thought they were born to be silent
With my brother they did nothing
but lie in the closet

I lifted them out
They poured out their secrets to me
They were open to mine, too
—when I spoke as a girl,
a mother, dancer, husband, thief,
they went with it

I carried them to new rooms, introduced them to new people,
brushed their hair and sometimes trimmed it

I changed their clothes and sang them to sleep
after we said prayers

I knew it was shameful for boys to play with dolls

—to make the lifeless feel beautiful,
kneeling beside them,
helping them rise and walk—

What kind of man would he grow up to be?

Miryam Buttons Yeshua's Coat

I'm five years old standing on the dunes
that slope toward the deepening water
The wind lashes my hood

The gray sky scours the beach
and keeps searching. Grass reaches
with never enough fingers
There are no birds, they have flown away
Shadows disappear from a sun
that has stormed off
The lone tree has roots
that drive through rock
and crack it. Waves push

But the wind suddenly stops,
whips its head around

It sees Mom kneeling
to button my coat

She concentrates on securing
the fabric into one calm shield
around my body,
ties my hood with a bow

A bird comes back, hovers
Sand puts down fistfuls
of glass and listens. Waves
crane their necks to see. The sun
does a double take, the slope
crawls up to watch

They've never seen anyone
make a center

Yeshua Chooses Seven Crayons

Why I Sit Beside Hana
Cutting out a shape
from construction paper,
Hana said,

My mom married a Matthias,
but I'll always be a Jacob

He Called Me Faggot
The sky
during recess
looks away

Starfish on the Beach
all the shells look exactly like millions of other remnants,
shells, but each remnant, each shell, once one thing's, just one
        thing's,
though in appearance like millions of others, how could that
        be, millions of laughters, millions of fears and ankles,

but only one Esther's ankles
only one James's ankles
how could that be how could that be
how could I have a mother

Reading
I bow to people that dream and fight,
people warm as summer, as biting as onions,
people that approach the deepest thing,
then veer off

Noah and the Ark
Verses lap across chapters
A ship sails an endless sea

My soul jumps up and down on the bow

There! And there!
My first language

Waves, waves
of silence

Learning to Write Cursive

I pour my attention into connecting

the bottom line

to the top line

with this line

Temple Camp

Our hair carries the scent of sea

into the chapel. We sit on the floor. I find pieces

of grass and stone hidden in the carpet,

roll them between my fingertips in the darkening light

We clap and stomp to the songs, and I love to sound

a little angry. After a song finishes, we hush. Solomon,

the tan counselor who plays guitar, chooses the next song

Let him, we each pray, choose mine

Yeshua Rides His Bike and Hears Life and Death

A leaf got caught in the spokes
I heard it whistling through the air as I rode
Then suddenly I didn't hear it
Where did it go   Where did it land
I don't know
There's no way to know

Yeshua Sits Cross-Legged with His Classmates and Listens to Artemis's Parable of the Soccer Match

At the soccer match
players kick the ball out of bounds
into the stands

The ball floats at you
It is big and soft. There is no way
you will not catch it

No one else in the stands moves to clutch it
They relax

That it is meant for you
is obvious

Just sit there

Who you are does not rise
and clamor for foul balls
that fly into the throng

The game is where you sit

and watch God's big, rounded softness
waft into your lap

Yeshua Watches a Street Artist Draw

The artist's drawing pad spread across his lap.

He sketched a house
in wide, fast pencil strokes.

One stroke unfurled stonework.
The next spilled
brick walks and archways

—the speed and effortlessness
by which a house
poured from his pencil
was the revelation

Yeshua Must Sit in Temple with the Boys

I was resentful about the rule:
boys sat on the left, girls sat on the right
Temple took me from my friends,
Hana and Ruthie
I felt separate from the boys too,
like a cat watching dogs
They stood on pews
or climbed underneath them,
pulling each other's laces,
sticking fingers into each other's ears
Shouldn't I be climbing and poking too?
But how loud the dome vibrated when I watched
its arc strum strings inside me. How loud Elijah's laugh
sheltered his fear. How obvious Daniel's dream
when he swatted Elijah and ducked
Not that my way of being in temple was more right or proper
than theirs
But mine was one path through the mountain
I, too, was a signpost
I, too, led a route across the mountain
of boy

Yeshua Resembles a Spectator Watching Olympic Figure Skaters Warm Up When He Watches Temple Debates

I stood against the wall lined with books
during temple debates, standing room only

like at the boards in the ice arena,
watching skaters stroke,
one push unleashing speed
for the triple Axel

The men were made
to leap, soar, and spin in the air,

to find the shining quotation
in the Torah and launch it
like a quadruple toe loop
from their lips

while competitors rested at the boards,
taking a sip of water,
turning Torah pages, the quad Lutz

waiting in their bodies,

about to spring

It was my secret

I belonged on the ice with them

I was the Olympic champion

who would never compete

Yeshua Meets God in the Double Lutz

Once every hundred attempts,
I do a perfect double Lutz

Launched into air,
I become God's sweet spot,
weightless inside forever

Heaven lasts for less than a second

before the blade lands on the ice
and taxis me back to Earth
But a passenger never forgets the flight
into Paradise

Why wait for death
to meet God?

I zoom around the rink
to try another double Lutz

Resurrection Begins after the Dance Concert

I was in the temple's dance company
and learned its choreography

—jabs and leaps, when to inhale and exhale,
when to enter stage left, what to wear

Yet I always had this worry: I sweated through my costume
Under stage lights, sweat spread like paw prints

across my butt and under my arms

I danced like a wave surging,
but with my back to the wall and elbows tucked in

After one performance, a woman came to me
in the lobby and said *You're only 75% alive*

Yeshua's Notes While Reading *The Epic of Gilgamesh*

Gilgamesh follows every emotion
to its limit

He reaches *the edge of the world*
and made his way back

His hands let go of weapons
and restore Eanna Temple

Resurrection is to decide
to think like God

What was ruined
wasn't

Yeshua's Friends Wait Outside while He Finishes Reading *Gilgamesh*

Gilgamesh falls in love like God does,
with everyone

Questions of preference
play no part in loving

Gilgamesh restores plazas and groves
for those whom he will never know,

criminals and victims alike

He rebuilds Eanna Temple
as a resurrection of innocence upon the highest hill

Each time we see another's innocence
we add weight to the grooved stone steps

to the temple

Yeshua Reads the Last Page of *Gilgamesh*. A Friend Tells Him to Hurry Up

Gilgamesh *at last arrived* where he began
He returns to his city,

walks markets and courtyards
His suffering—mountain trek

and ocean storm; love leashed, then not
—evaporates

The story is not to have a story

Beginning and ending
the same place

Yeshua Wonders if He'd Consider Gilgamesh a Messiah

The Messiah could be anyone willing
to make their life's work

a change of perspective,
the decision to climb stairs

to the temple of the mind
and separate—as a livelihood—

fear
from God

Yeshua Borrows the *Iliad* from Rabbi's Library

My favorite character:
neither Greek hero Achilles
nor his Trojan rival Hector,
but Homer,
the writer,
who stands outside war
like God

Homer takes off Achilles's armor
and perches him as a toddler
upon his adoptive father Phoenix's knee
Achilles slobbers meat spittle
onto Phoenix's shoulder,
who wipes the child's cheeks
with a napkin

Trojan Hector is not an enemy,
but a father
He cradles his son upon his lap to enjoy
the choicest morsel

Hand's motion from man's plate
to toddler's mouth as Greek as it is Trojan

Roman soldiers humiliate my uncles—
My uncles mock Roman soldiers—
Their cheeks are so soft
inside. They all deserve a father
pulling them to the table
to be fed the best meat

Homer
cuts venison
into mouth-sized pieces
for Greek sons, for Trojan sons.
He brushes their hair back
with the palm of the hand,
wipes each mouth with soft cloth

Yeshua Wonders When His Edge Will Come

The Greek king shames Achilles
in front of the entire brigade
Achilles chokes back tears
until he is out of sight,
runs to the coastline, drops to his knees
sobbing, snot dripping into
his heaving mouth
He does not realize he calls for his mother,
Thetis, a Goddess who flies to him,
his forehead caked
with sweat and sand

Mother and God, no distinction
They hear where the son's world ends

The *Iliad* Ends with Sworn Enemies Sobbing Together

In the poem's final scene, sunk at the bottom
of 1000 pages of men raging,
is sadness

That's where sworn enemies meet,
King Priam and warrior Achilles
They weep

Guards marvel,
shocked by the strength of male
sobs, how quickly shirts darken
with drool

Start here, Homer says,
at the end, when we're on our knees,
and we've forgotten
we're supposed to take a stand

Tears blur edges between you
and me, right and wrong, and we see
only soft shapes softer, and that, finally,

is vision

Yeshua Rereads the *Iliad*'s Final Line. It Speaks to Something Deep Inside Him

"And so the Trojans buried Hector breaker of horses."

– Homer's The Iliad

Only young Hector,
irreplaceable prince,
visits the horses

In their eyes' sharp unreason,
he sees his own. He sees God's still,
dark pool

Hector cups oats
Apple slices. Cubes of sugar
Approaches sidelong the muzzle,
holds dates to the mouth
that will never thank him,
so hungrily the lips devour sweets

Yeshua Begins to Understand the Greek Gods

My three-year-old nephew Ezekiel wanted another cookie
We had just finished lunch

My dad, gathering dishes, replied,
"Ezekiel, you've already had a cookie"

Ezekiel leaned forward
His forehead made lines: *I don't think you understand*

He tried again. "I want a cookie. Please"

My brother James had relocated outside
Mom was bringing dishes to the sink

A storm broke in Ezekiel's eyes

"Did you fix Rabbi's chair?" my dad asked me

Ezekiel looked upward from height to height,
Grandpa, Grandma, and me

Sky between clouds

I just watched

Yeshua Interviews Hebrew, Egyptian, Greek, and Mesopotamian Gods for a Research Project on Interfaith Dialogue

Do we take language too seriously?

[Nothing]

Well, does fear accompany truth?

[Nothing]

The real tension is between love and grammar, right?

[Nothing]

I think each individual is the answer.

[Nothing]

Are you even real? Where do you live?

[Little laugh]

Finally, a response.

[Two cats sleeping in the sun]

Was the laugh I heard sunlight? The cats? You?

[Nothing]

I guess the interview is over.

[If you say so, my Love

      —or the day sky overfull with stars]

Yeshua Reflects on Yosef's Architectural Aesthetic

My dad likes simple roofs. The more angles and corners,
the more pressure points needing repair

This explains the soul's longevity. It has no angles or corners,
no walls to uphold. Unlike the heart, soul never strains

It does no work

God's architectural aesthetic is like my dad's, but with slat
        boards
removed, ceilings opened, and floors rolled back

Think of a temple cleared of pillars and altars
Stone steps dusted away

A place to wake up into the most delicious sleep
with no dreams

Yeshua Does Not Yet Want to Drop Carpentry

God wants walls down. I make him a window
with my hammer

God wants walls down. I make him a door
with my good hammer

God wants walls down

He points to sky and sea
as examples

I make him another window
with a screen
using my best hammer

God wants walls down
I consider dropping carpentry

Yeshua Notices Tree Yoga

A tree

inhaling

exhaling

      being God's answer
      without
      believing it

The Woman at the Well Watches Yeshua while Experts Lecture Him

She said to Yeshua, "I can see that you are a prophet."

—John 4:19 (NIV)

Yeshua sits silently, nodding
as if he were a student to their lecture

though he thinks from wells
wider than their tight philosophies

I wonder if I look like him
when men explain to me how to draw water

from a well whose bucket I lower and raise
multiple times a day, my fingerprints covering the wet,

fraying rope, traces of myself
reaching rock bottom

A Mystic Doesn't Yet Know She is One

Heaven and Earth
splash inside my eyeballs

Shells spill upon the shore,
bursts of disappearance
everywhere visible

Maybe I should learn finance,
post on social media, or march in the uprising

But God never takes His cupped hands
from my ear

or lets me leave
His mind

Yeshua Notices a Turtle while His Friends Remonstrate Against Injustices

Eternity is the hard shell that encases you

You wake and sleep within it

Whether you stretch your limbs in joy
or draw them back in fear,
your core is safe

as you trek across the path,
disappear into the pond,
swim buoyant as air

Roman Occupation Does Not Bother
Yeshua as Much as It Bothers His Friends

Live like you are dead
in peace that nothing can threaten
—war, sickness, pride, desire, nothing

Grasp for nothing because nothing is needed
Defend nothing because nothing is attacked

Enveloped in love and patience
unchanging
live as though you were dead

When you die nothing happens
but the life you were living

Yeshua Gets Help Finding the Temple

I walked to the temple retreat in Jerusalem
carrying my bag of food and clothes
My first trip to the city alone

The path diverged into two
Atop the hill, I saw the paths connect
again beyond gardens and plazas

But on my map, the paths stayed separated
One continued right, and the other continued left
Should I trust my eyes or the map?

I stepped inside a shop to ask for help

A clerk looked up from his repair table
He was shirtless except for a vest
opened across his chest, glistening
with sweat from his labor

How can I help you

I told him I was looking for the temple,
but was confused

Should I trust my eyes or the map

Moonlight escaped from his eyes
like stars through woods,
a folded map in the sky

The temple's not far, he said
I'll bring you there

Could he just leave his workplace like that?
But I sensed his job
was to show me
the temple

Yeshua Enjoys a Night Out in Jerusalem

I ate the cherries,

but only the ones that spilled out of the basket

Yeshua Focuses on One Cherry

I practiced gratitude for one cherry
It dangled on a stem, making itself easy
for me to take
I could tell it desired my tug
because it dropped from the branch
when I barely touched it
I held it before my eyes by the stem,
it shined its naked skin for me,
its curves just the size of my open lips
In my mouth, it splashed its juice instantly,
eager to share its wet sweetness
with my one, raucous tongue, my one smooth
throat. Its everything inched toward my heart

Yet not everything
The cherry shared one thing I spit out
without thinking:
its very center

Yeshua Explains How Getting PrEP as a Young Adult Influenced His Ministry

I had run out of my medication
Apothecaries in Nazareth didn't carry the taboo pills
My supplier wouldn't have more for another month
until he went to Jerusalem

A quiet woman at temple
pulled me aside after service,
told me to visit a Sister Susan
who would be expecting me
at 10:45 p.m. in the old temple's basement
The woman's eyes sparkled. Then
she left to serve cookies in the lobby

I arrived at the old temple,
walked down a dank staircase, passed
men with crutches who hadn't changed shirts
in a lifetime. I asked a woman bandaging a man's foot
I wouldn't look at
if she knew where I could find Sister Susan

She pointed with her chin. *Last door on the left*

I paused in the open doorframe. Sister Susan turned around,
put the bottle on the desk
and said, I'm just going to leave this here

She continued her conversation
with a woman holding a clipboard and taking notes

I took the bottle

A thin man whose eyes were dead
or on eternity watched me
or nothing as I climbed the stairs
and left

It dawned on me that the woman serving cookies
was Sister Susan's disciple

Or Sister Susan was hers

And the woman with the clipboard was writing their gospel

Reading *Frankenstein*, Yeshua Considers His Demon

You look like a monster
But you're telling me you're an angel

You're telling me to drop blame, shame, and fame

You're telling me to drop my life
And then I'll be who I am

You sound crazy

Yeshua Wakes

I woke from the dream

The artist hadn't entrusted his masterpiece to me
The wind hadn't torn it from my hands and thrashed it down
the street

The artist did not exist
Nor did his masterpiece
My shame for failing them, as unreal as they

Yeshua's Dreams Tell Him to Grow Up

My dreams began telling me to go away

All the cups on the counter: none of them were mine
I stood in doorways flung open to swept, tidy rooms

Don't come closer,
my dreams told me

Leave
Go where you're not dreaming

Hana Reminds Yeshua that God Sends Angels to Spread His Heresy

1.

Angels long for heresy

Gabriel, for instance, named
your parents' pre-marital sex
divine

2.

In a storm
others hear windows shake and winds howl

You hear differences between bronzed terraces and dirt floors,
between sacred tablets and throwaway scraps
disappear under rising glitter

You watch while everyone runs for latches and doors, brooms
       and buckets

They're inflamed you're not helping

You help them
let light
pile

Why Yeshua Left Nazareth

I considered staying in my hometown
and becoming a rabbi in sleepy Nazareth

The magnitude of its temple was unequalled for miles
with a soaring tower atop the grand brick entrance
Windows arched above stone steps ascending
to a portico that spanned the façade

But the temple had fallen into disrepair
No one assembled in its yard
for market or gathered on its terrace
for coffee. I imposed ghosts
I wanted there: scents of perfume
and musk, chairs for artists and seekers
to people-watch, flirt, and share stories
on paper, in paint, and in person.
The building stood with skin fallen off
A skeleton

My father came with me to look at the place—
to see, one last time, if I might turn the temple around

Inside, the walls were bare except for chipped paint
Old buckets stood in the lobby
The grand hall, wide open for flirting, empty
Smell of closets no one had opened for decades

The skeleton lifted its finger
and pointed me away
to the city

Jerusalem

A Lover Remembers Yeshua

Yeshua brought God to the bed, against the wall,
across the table

Sacred tablets fell to the ground,
crashed, split into a million pieces

God, scattered everywhere—

I worried that we couldn't put Him back together again

Leave Him like that, Yeshua said
That's how He likes it

Yeshua Remembers the Dock at the Sea of Galilee

Some men gathered for communion under the dock
very late, at a sacred hour when the moon
coaxed the world quiet

Some worshippers were fishermen, some carpenters
Others were Pharisees or Sadducees,
travelers or teachers,
Samaritans and Judeans,
Syrians

Some knelt in the sand
Others stood

as the sound of lapping waves
warmed eyes, hearts,
and lips open

From a distance
passersby might see
eyes sparkling in the darkness
and think men were walking on water

Yeshua Rereads *Gilgamesh*. Ponders Shamhat, the Sex Worker

The gods are tired of Gilgamesh's tyranny
and create Enkidu to overthrow him

But first, Enkidu meets Shamhat

After they make love, Shamhat
tells Enkidu her dream

She sees Gilgamesh hold and caress
him like a wife

Enkidu neither questions nor resists

when Shamhat walks him to Gilgamesh
then leaves them alone
to enter her dream

Walking to the Wedding, Yeshua Stops in the Street

Gilgamesh was on his way to a wedding
He liked to barge in
before the groom to take the bride first

That's him, Shamhat says to Enkidu
Go, she says with her eyes

Enkidu intercepts Gilgamesh
and declares, Oh no you don't, Gilgamesh.
Not on my watch

The two men seize each other,
roll and grab, grunt and moan
in the dirt, which widens into a bed
they're surprised to find they don't want to leave
Biceps flex into shy gifts, hands find sculpture
down the back, breath dangles on the tip
of eyelash brushing eyelash

Men loving their enemies

Yeshua stops in the street

    I want to bring Shamhat's dream
    back to public square

Why Yeshua Changed Water to Wine

At the wedding, the groom's brother
sat beside me on the stone wall bordering the garden
where everyone danced and drank

The music held us apart from them like a soft net
He was drunk and moving his body close to mine

His knee touched mine
He moved the insides of his eyes
closer to the insides of my eyes.

He said, The wine is nearly out
One more sip pooled in his glass
His eyes mouthed

Kiss me

I got up, found the barrels, and turned water to wine
not for the bride and groom,

but for the changes wine works in a man

to ache so tenderly, so openly

for a kiss in a garden

Yeshua Guesses Deuteronomy's Writer Had Never Been Kissed by a Man from Sodom

For their vine comes from the vine of Sodom and from the fields of Gomorrah; their grapes are grapes of poison; their clusters are bitter.

— Deuteronomy 32:32 (NIV)

Mid-morning market

Banners, not yet tired,

burst splendor in the air

like grapes overflowing across tables

People balanced drinks in both hands,

vendors passed figs and lentils to

shoppers, others rested in Temple Square

listening to harps, drums, and rumbling carts

Children ran ahead of parents, teenagers flirted, and something
    long sleeping in dogs

awakened in jasmine-chai air

It started to rain, and shrieks of delight

rose from shoppers as they ran for cover,

palms to God, laughing and praising His goodness

I dashed under a storefront portico

and watched passersby clamber

into carts or throw open tent flaps

which dropped behind them

The world was wet like a bathing suit

Some young men crowded

into the portico beside me, bringing scents of damp linen

and wine. I could tell they were

from Sodom by their accents and the ways

their beards glistened like where the Jordan bends

and the current changes

One man shouted to another friend

on the street to bring the cart. The men darted

out, heads ducked, laughing, spilling

their mugs of wine

One man lingered in the portico. He stepped toward me

and asked May I kiss you?

Yes

Two rain drops fell onto two rain drops

Then he leapt out of the portico
and jumped into the cart behind his friends
It sped into the splashing air. Tables
overflowed with grapes

Maybe Deuteronomy's Writer *Had* Been Kissed by a Man from Sodom

Kissed by him many times, under trees along the brook,

in the barn loft, in the secluded lane outside the Temple

And then Deuteronomy's writer—let's call him, say,
       Benjamin—

sees his lover from Sodom

kiss another man in a portico

during a sudden rainstorm

at market

That his lover from Sodom

shared the grapes on that vine

so perfectly shaped for Benjamin's lips,

that all it took was a stranger

caught in a rainstorm at market

for the man from Sodom to share a sweetness

so perfectly lapped by his, Benjamin's, tongue,

was the bitterness that burned Benjamin's blood,
the heat that incinerated his veins, the poisonous fumes
seeped into his mind,

everyone else scattered and laughing,
their palms lifted to heaven and praising God's gifts
from impromptu shelters, except for Benjamin,

whose lips should be being kissed
in a portico, but who instead
stood in the pouring rain

Man from Sodom Explains Resurrection

Whenever I am naked and not ashamed,
I am back in the Garden of Eden,
resurrected into innocence,
my true being

Whenever I am naked in bed with another man,
I bring him to Eden, too. We return each other to God,
skin to skin through the gate
and down the path to Paradise

I often don't know the man's name
I don't need to know
We're before Adam,
and Eve,
before man
and woman,
before names and animals,
before sea and sky,
before light,
in the beginning

just God all
night

Yeshua Walks into the Garden of Eden

So the Lord God banished [Adam] from the Garden of Eden .
. . and placed . . . cherubim and a flaming sword flashing back
and forth to guard the way to the tree of life.

—Genesis 3:24 (NIV)

Step off the road
Duck under branches,
walk into clover
Watch the river ripple like silk
Trees and brush on the other side
lie like pillows on a bed as
wide as the landscape. The sloshing water
or lovers' lips kiss mineral, kiss
root. Plenty of space to lie down
on a blanket or roll off beside trees,
thick bedposts. The Garden of Eden's
gate stands wide open
right now. There are no angels and sword barring the way
I simply stepped off the path
as it began to rain

The Bridegroom Shares a Secret

The bridegroom was a long time in coming, and they all
became drowsy and fell asleep. At midnight the cry rang out:
"Here's the bridegroom! Come out to meet him!"

—Matthew 25:5-6 (NIV)

I was at the rock with Jeremiah
We carved our initials into our stone

just past the fence over the hill
twenty-seven paces from the Temple

The night was humid. We dripped with sweat
I pressed my hands against the rock

to etch, while pulling the strain
back into my body to stop sweating

into the wedding shirt
my mother had made

When I stepped back the letters
looked like *If*

and I was horrified to see
holes in my shirt

but they were patches of sweat

The Groom's Sister Does Not Bring Oil for Her Candle

Ten virgins took their lamps and went out to meet the
bridegroom. The foolish ones took their lamps but did not
take any oil with them. The foolish ones said to the wise,
"Give us some of your oil; our lamps are going out."

—Matthew 25:1-3 (NIV)

Look at him arriving sweaty with Jeremiah
Sorry, sorry they say

I saw the oil on the counter at home
and left it

I let my oil run dry

Mornings before work, my brother would make two
lunches, one for himself, one
for Jeremiah

I'll honor those early hours
with my candle that won't light

and stand almost unnoticeable

like two handfuls of extra figs
Mom set on the counter each night

Yeshua Dances at the Wedding

I waft my wrists
softer. Softer.
Tenderness only looks easy

Gods withhold harvest, rainfall, a lover?
I am that for which I long
for as long as I dance

Kindling in my thighs
Forehead moistens like a cloud
Eternity lasts for as long as I want it

My arm. Yours. Ours
Ancestors dance me. Resurrection
is not a miracle. It's ordinary
Move

Grandma died?
Dance
Gilgamesh died?
Dance

They're still dead?

Dance again

I died?

Someone's dancing

Yeshua Asks a Stranger at the Gym If He's Finished Using the Squat Rack

Often when I speak to strangers
I cannot believe "Hello" or "Excuse me"
comes out of my mouth and the person
understands. They answer with
"Mhmm" or "All yours" – and I understand
them. I wonder how this happened, how did I rise
from the soul and ask to share a piece of
equipment at the gym or squeeze past a shopper in the aisle

Where am I? I'm shocked
like a chipmunk when I see I'm not
in the soul's burrow, but I calm when I see
I haven't gone far, just to "Hello" or "Excuse me"
or to pick up a dumbbell

Yeshua Loves the Outdoor Gym in Jerusalem

The Good Samaritan's name was Joel,

and the assaulted man thrown in the ditch whom he helped
was David

Joel recognized David from the public, outdoor gym

in Jerusalem where some of us worked out

Egyptians. Sumerians. Judeans. Samaritans

Were it not for the outdoor gym, our windows would've

stayed rolled up to each other, our shirts buttoned up like our
hearts,

ear buds in. Under the sky, we mimicked its openness,

speaking its language of shirts off. We tucked them

into our shorts for wiping sweat. We squatted under dip bars

and moaned over high bars, sweat shimmering like body-sized
suns across our backs and down the dip of buttocks

We enjoyed a nakedness,

an intimacy, pushing our bodies beyond their limits,

together—not only fathers, sons, and husbands,

but muscles and tendons of sun and cloud through eight, nine,

ten chin-ups, rolling over to rest. Life is work
for each of us. We're breathless with each other

This gym is a training space for paradise
We practice expanding our range of motion: one more rep
     beyond
our comfort level. Doing pull-ups, we reach toward sky
Impossible to make it, but for an hour we move
in that direction. I gain strength to stall an eye roll
longer than I thought I ever could
when mansplainers lecture me

When Joel, the Samaritan, saw David in the ditch,
     he moved his muscles
from walking to helping, greater range of motion
than the priest and Levite had,
who passed David by on their way to the city's
air-conditioned gym with double doors
that closed behind them

Yeshua Checks Out Fire Island

I considered renting a place on the island

I looked at a manicured
plot of land decorated with a new
tree. Fresh mulch encircled
its base, equidistance immaculate,
or careful. The grass was cut and verdant,
or shiny

The owner took out his measuring tape
See? – he showed me on his tape,
more than enough space
He stood back, proud

The grass shined
all the way to the woods
then stopped

The measuring tape
in my soul shook its head no

Yeshua Remembers an Incident Involving Poetry

Two friends started
a community writing workshop

Some participants wrote men kissing men
into their poems and stapled their work
into prayer journals

One morning a writer showed me
a journal: the poems had been ripped out

Heading home, I saw a mob
swarming toward my apartment
brandishing journals and torn poems

God opens like a drawer

and opens again like a folded scrap of paper
at the back of the drawer

and opens like a word
on the scrap

Yeshua Chats with a Person Who is About to Torch and Riot Downtown

We think God knows everything, but He doesn't

He doesn't know how to post on social media
or how to drive. He can't figure out
handcuffs or how to set a building on fire

If we narrowed our area of expertise
to Nonsensical Peace, Absurd Love,
and Everyone-is-Innocent,

we'd know as little as God does

A Protestor Remembers Yeshua Adoring Stones instead of Throwing Them

I stood beside Yeshua at the revolt
I remember him picking up a rock
and turning it in his fingers

Swirls of darks and lights, he said
Atmospheric insides
Maelstrom stillness forever
Ground Star,
your life is hard

Yeshua Remembers the Silence after a Lover Breaks Up with Him

Friends told me the beloved *sucked,*
A.'s a jerk and doesn't deserve you

But Eros had given me kaleidoscopic vision

Each of my beloved's eyelashes
splashed different shades of onyx
like canoes ashore in moonlight

I now discerned lines of light
shifting across strangers' clavicles and lips

I saw friends' eyes glisten the same gold
as their upper lips when they cupped

—almost kissing—

the word "jerk"

Saddle-brown with a hint of dusk-lavender
moved across a vendor's cheek while he passed figs
to octagons of obsidian-rose, a customer's hand

I learned to call resplendence "Philip" or "Mary,"
"Caesar" or "Samaritan"
for others to understand whom I meant

Jade-blue faded into delphinium-mint,
or a mansplainer's eyes as he lectured me

Moon-pearl, or the soldier's forearms
who placed me in handcuffs,

his stubble shimmering like his eyes
must have when he was a little boy

allowed to choose his favorite sweet
from a basket

Yeshua Reflects on His Last Supper Cup

My dad had come into the kitchen
asking if any of us had seen his cup,

the one that had belonged to his father, now passed away

My dad drank tea from it every morning

Every time he drank,
he brought Grandpa back to life

The dead and the living became one motion

—clasping the handle—lips cupping ceramic—
the same spilling-warmth down the throat

*

No, I didn't know where his cup was

My aunt barely raised her head from her writing. No, she
didn't know either

My brother gave a *No* on his way out the door

We never found the cup

*

Years later, after my dad had passed away, I discovered the cup
filled with sand behind a tree in the backyard

A niece must've used it to build a fort

I took it. Drank tea from it the next morning. Then the next.
Then every morning. I carried the cup with me to Jericho,
Canaan, Jerusalem

My father returned at 8 a.m. when I clasped the handle.
Cupped my fingers around warmth the width of his forearm

Drank

I brought the cup to the last supper. Raised it to my lips to
explain eternal life

Yeshua's Unborn Baby Speaks to Him

Do not pull me away from God into your self

Keep me unborn

Learn from me

to be unborn again

Yeshua's Grandpa Sits Him Down. Again

Yeshua.

You need to settle down.

Buy some property.

Marry.

You're not young anymore.

You've never known what it's like to love.

Yeshua Often Doubts What He Knows

I test myself | no test

Test again | no test

| you passed before you passed

I didn't pass again | no test

A test to make sure I pass | dawn. rain

I look to others to see if I pass | God

I look to others | God

I, others | God

Eye to eye | God

I didn't pass again | God

No test? | upswelling inborn fountain

I see you, eye to eye? | upswelling inborn fountain

no test | upswelling inborn fountain

I passed | upswelling inborn fountain

this bouquet, yours for nothing,
blossoms of white on white,
black on black

Yeshua Resurrects When He Should be Debating

Whenever I decide
to rise above the battle

—right attacking wrong,
wrong clobbering right,
and their shared mania against peace—

the rock rolls away
I step from the tomb
I stand in the garden
I am risen indeed

Yeshua Can Still Hear Yohanan the Baptist's Voice as if It Were Yesterday

I could sit in the river
forever with the sun

Study light play
with depths and shallows

Float and sink

Hover my palms over
smooth rocks

The sound of almost nothing

I decided to make this my life

Yeshua Wades in the Bay

I dug up shells
Long ones wound tight,
flat ones open like a diary
in candlelight, broken ones
with edges sharp and smooth
Some carried strange holes
Some streaked with purple or gold,
splashes of rose, as if they dreamed
wildflower into their skin
We each are sea
Wade in yourself
No need to go deep. Even in the shallow ends
you'll pull up ancient ceramics
that confirm your private dream

Yeshua Sees Poseidon

I was swimming in the sea
and I saw him:
shirtless, long hair wet
over his shoulders
Seated, even lounging
Small. He floated above the waves,
which covered my view of him
as he moved in and out of my sight
He was more muscular
than average, but normal
Tired, but youthful, alert
He looked far away toward something inside

The Lake is Like God

The lake stands
gleaming, dark

Toward nightfall, after dinner and dishes,
after emails and homework,
after sex or before, but always before sleep,
people walk to the lake

People in love and second graders,
teachers, parents who know their children
are bullies, the secret bullies, former prisoners,
someone who will be in prison. Their
victims, their mothers, someone
who knows their naked chest and thinks about them
naked when they themselves are naked. Someone
who voted left. Who voted right
Someone forgotten. The first red leaf in autumn
A greyhound. Someone suddenly remembered

Begin here:

How none of us go into the lake
How closely we gather together
around the edge

Yeshua's Spiritual Journey

For all those who exalt themselves will be humbled, and those who humble themselves will be exalted.

— Luke 18-14 (NIV)

The mansplainer in my parable? That's me,
self-congratulatory in o how holy I am
I'm not like the story's tax collector whose eyes are on the
        prize
Until they are. I want to win first place for God

When I see that the mansplainer is the tax collector
is myself, I ask God
to heal me. He rolls out space between me
and the pride and shame I kneel to

I'm getting better
at staying on my knees when I want to jump up
and catch the pride and shame blowing away
down God's windy space

Yeshua Watches a Composer Conduct His New Piece with the Orchestra

The composer lives in his mind
He listens to harp strings raise palaces
as he walks to market,
zig zags around carts while horns honk
and protestors shout. I heard he did not join the uprising

And now we gather to listen to flutes
he sensed in solitude among carpenters sawing
and children racing to school. The tremolo he nearly did not
    trace
The melody his ears almost closed to, convinced
true tones repeat shouts and swinging signs
across public square

In the audience, we watch in silence his silence
We watch how he changes
when he is silent

The musicians practiced the news he allowed himself
to note. Chords he allowed himself, finally, to rearrange

We were waiting for his sforzandos we never knew we wanted,
waiting to store the revolt and put the sign away
for this sound bouquet, to hear trumpets
he eventually let sound, but barely
So unspeakable that major chord

Our ears insert the key let loose from
his small hands and slight arms. Every door opens

This music nods *Yes*, says *Go ahead*
The beats you're skipping over, the rondo you let
disappear under rumbling wheels and revolutions

Yes, that one

Look. It is done
Go away, alone, into your mind
Come back often and play for us the pianissimos
you heard, the up risings we nearly missed

Mary Magdalene Looks into the Tomb and Corrects Herself

Instead of securing a stone between death and myself,
I shook myself out of the self's doormat

Floating away, I saw other pieces loosened
like dust wafting

That's when I saw the gardener,
an angel,
myself

—dust struck
by sunlight and shimmering in the air

Our thinking was our shimmering

Mary Magdalene Sits Down for Coffee with a Fellow Writer at the Conference

John writes that Thomas touched
Jesus's hands after he rose from the tomb

That's John's version
Thomas's is different

Thomas loved Jesus, so he didn't care
whether Jesus did impressive things
like rise from the dead and walk

Maybe John needed Jesus's physical hand
to understand resurrection

Some people need proof that the heart
is an organ of sight, or seek a formula for reincarnation in the
chemical composition of oxygen bubbles

Other people hear a grandfather's voice
in a grandson's and say, "Eternal life. Got it"

How we remember our beloveds is artistic license
John loved Jesus so much he couldn't let him go

It can be hard for a man to admit that ache
for another man's hand. So John had Thomas hold it

A Conference Participant Asks John Why
He Wrote So Many Books About Jesus

Consensus never exists in a sentence

s needs more curves than *j* does. They bend at different places

e's loop is a different temperament than *o*'s

a wonders why *b* reaches so high when everything is right here

b wonders why *a* stops when there's so much more

l escorts me to life then hands me to *i*

t is too scared to see the other side of death so it leans on *h*

Avoiding conclusions is sacred work

As soon as I make a decision about God
I write another sentence

Jesus Sits Down to Draft His Paper for the Teachers Conference

Maria Montessori once said

Don't look at me

Look at where I'm pointing

A Reader Asks Jesus What He Thinks about the New Testament

Reading the New Testament is like this:

Teachers have invited me to visit their school
I'm excited to see students' drawings of choirs wearing
    colorful robes,
to eat lunch with teachers in the courtyard

I run up to the school entrance
The security guard pulls out a gun
Hands up! he shouts
The manual states everyone is a potential threat

I stretch my arms upward
through my fingertips
I stretch each leg and point my toes

The guard searches me,
pats down my chest and hips,
turns me around to get my back and thighs
He sits me on the floor,

then sits down behind me

His legs and torso cup my body

I see his badge from the corner of my eye

as he rubs his hands up and down my arms

and speaks softly into my ear,

    It's ok, you're good, have fun,

still spooning me

Jesus Heals a Gay Man

I heard Jesus healed people with evil spirits

He would walk into public gatherings, touch the afflicted, and rebuke the demon,

exclaiming, I command you, come out of him and never enter him again!

I knew he was to visit my temple for Passover

I arrived amid the buzz, temple leaders asking if Jesus needed anything to eat or drink

Later in the din of moving tables and chairs, I noticed quiet. The others had gone to the yard

Jesus and I were alone, unfolding tablecloths

My feet moved me toward him, my brow moistened

I need to be healed, I whispered. From a demon

He cocked his head, moved his ear to hear more. I could feel
him listening through his warm cheek

I have a devil in me —
I —
I don't want a   wife

—the demon clawed my throat

I want

                                        —shame choked my
reddening face

Would he throw down the tablecloth, spit into my eyes, look
up to heaven with horrified rebuke?

But he just lifted another corner

Lots of my friends will be at the feast tonight, he said,
flapping the cloth like a sail billowing across the table

I can introduce you to some, he added, smoothing bumps in
the cloth

Mary's Biographer Reflects on Three Ceramic Shoes

In Mary's home, beside her bed,
three little ceramic, decorative shoes line her windowsill

I was not going to ask her about them,
assuming they represent her three children: Jesus, James, and
      Esther

But they don't

She said they stand for her siblings:
Rose, herself, and Noah, who died as an infant

When Mary rises every morning, the first thing she sees
is this trio, with one member always missing

But no, she corrected me, *missing* is wrong too

We all lead full lives

Peter's Nephew Shows Jesus Real Life

Truly I tell you, unless you change and become like little
children, you will never enter the kingdom of heaven.

—Matthew 18:2-4 (NIV)

My Uncle Peter and Jesus talked
late into the night, wine glasses full and bottles empty

I lay on the floor playing with toy soldiers,
zooming them across moonlight pooling on the mat,

my imaginary sea. *Splash*
I whispered to myself   *Splash*

Jesus laughed. "Your men are fine swimmers!"

"No, they're walking." I showed him

"But men can't walk on water," Jesus responded

"Why not?" I insisted

"They'd sink"

I'd never been to the sea

"They don't sink," I said. "Mom says
we're always safe in God's hands. See?"

I walked a man from one side of the moonlit mat to the other

A Widow Explains How Jesus Raised Her Son from the Dead

"Young man, I say to you, get up!" The dead man sat up and began to talk, and Jesus gave him back to his mother.

—Luke 7:15 (NIV)

Jesus touched my son's coffin,
the hardened idea of death
I had let congeal around my life

Had I put my son into that idea?
Had I killed my son?
Was it I who kept him dead?
Was it true I would rather choose death than God?

I stopped crying to listen

Every time I was willing to hear
my son's silence instead of the coffin's
he came back

A Stoic and His Daughter Listen to the Apostle Paul

Paul tells Athenians, "We should not think that the divine being is like gold or silver or stone—an image made by man's design and skill."

—Acts 17:29 (NIV)

1. The Stoic

Paul, we are both listeners
to the soul's first language

We hear the same silence
–light splashing across stones
like the one you treasure in your pocket
from a road in Damascus

2. The Stoic's Daughter

Paul speaks of the Good News
It sounds like old news to me

A man telling me what to believe
without bothering to ask

what I believe, because it is wrong

So he will never know
what he believes is wrong

I have never once thought the divine being
is an image made by man's design and skill

Athena
Help

Jesus Tries to Go to Church This Morning

I never made it because I didn't realize you needed a driver's
    license
I started to walk but the sidewalks ran out
Suddenly it was just me standing on the side of the road
and cars whizzing past at 55+ mph

Apparently they've made two ways to God
You can drive down Northfield or Eastbranch
You have to get a car before you get God
People speed to church without me
Parking lots are bigger than churches

I never mentioned cars during my ministry,
but people brought them to church like food for a feast
I never mentioned gay or transgender folks during my
    ministry,
but people avoid them like germs

Clearing more space for cars than for people
reminded me of McDonalds drive-thrus

I tried to buy a drink from there once,
but they said I needed a car
before they'd serve me
so I left

Bible Art

Each of God's children
is a different chime
the same word
hits

The Podcast Host Asks Jesus to Explain Again Because Listeners Want to Understand

I can use a wrench
and fix doors just fine

But the tools that come naturally
to me are introspection
and patience with discomfort

I noticed cracked souls
more than creaking doors

I was ashamed of that skill for a long time
because I didn't think it was one

I looked so deeply into everyone
I fixated on their fundamental innocence

I knew I was supposed to be mad at injustices like everybody
     else
but I wasn't, because everyone—violated and violator—is
     innocent

We are The Same from eternity's perspective
Eternity is the Great Equalizer

I decided to function at the level of eternity

When you see everyone as God underneath fear's gunk
you can't take sides. Eternity has no left and right

When they come to kill you, as they did for me,
you see eternity, not men carrying weapons

I could not fear eternity
coming for eternity

It would've been like a fish
fearful of water

Jesus Gives the Keynote Address at the National Speech & Debate Tournament

Growing up, boys had to speak up to win God

Fathers wanted sons in Debate League
I joined and practiced announcing
loopholes in other's arguments
Gotcha for God

But I was not selected for the Young Debaters

I was more listener
I stood back
and heard
a whisper of suffering
in the farthest corners of the winning arguments

Only later did I recognize that listening is
not disappearance but emergence

Pausing to listen loosens a mist
that obscures golden domes from ramshackle roofs

Now everyone can come out
about cracks and water damage

People remember me as a healer of leprosy, demons, and even
        death
Really I just listened,

patient with the odor of unwashed hair
and with eyes watering from Hell's heat

I thought leprosy, demons, and death were worth listening to
and not defeating

Jesus Agrees He's Not Fully Human

I was a lake
that absorbed stones
without rippling

I was Being
—the part in us we have to let go
for it to fly

I practiced boarding flight more and more
I eventually flew whenever I wanted to

When people threw rocks—words, spit, thorns—
I had already taken off

At my trial everyone was confused

I looked like a man
but was a lake

The gleam
—my skin or sky

Jesus's Parable of the Windy Day

The street artist watched the wind take his drawing

It flapped across the ground and past street vendors
The artist did not yell to passersby to catch it

Nonetheless, a couple of men tried, even climbing up a fire
    escape to follow it
blowing upward past the second floor

That is the self, blowing away, Jesus said
People tried to rescue mine by writing the Gospels

Luke, John, even B. climbed that fire escape
They think I lost something precious

I was the artist who stood there and watched it blow away

Notes

"Preface: A Queer Gospel in Poetry" — Quotations derive from the following three books: Willis Barnstone's *The Poems of Jesus Christ* (W. W. Norton & Company, 2012), John Shelby Spong's *Resurrection: Myth or Reality? A Bishop's Search for the Origins of Christianity* (HarperCollins, 1994), and Mircea Eliade's *The Sacred and the Profane: The Nature of Religion* (Harcourt, 1987). All quotations are used with permission.

"Yeshua Realizes He is Miryam" — The concept for this poem owes a debt to poet Pádraig Ó Tuama, who shares, "At about 2:00 in the morning, I . . . walked about three miles to the ocean. . . . There was a big statue of Mary out by this particular beach— and [I] just shouted out, 'Are there any other people like me around?' And I was so lonely and so desperate and felt so completely alone" (*On Being*'s "Poetry Unbound" podcast episode featuring Kei Miller's poem "Book of Genesis," original air date March 6, 2020, *OnBeing.org*).

"One of the Wise Men Explains Why He Became an Astronomer" — Anu is King of the Gods and Lord of the Constellations in ancient Mesopotamia.

"Yeshua Sits Cross-Legged with His Classmates and Listens to Artemis's Parable of the Soccer Match" — Artemis is the Greek goddess of athletics, hunting, wild nature, and virginity.

"Yeshua Meets God in the Double Lutz"— the Lutz is the name of a specific jump in figure skating, named after its Austrian inventor, Alois Lutz.

"Yeshua's Notes While Reading *The Epic of Gilgamesh*," "Friends Wait Outside While He Finishes Reading *Gilgamesh*," "Yeshua Reads the Last Page of *Gilgamesh*. A Friend Tells Him to Hurry Up," "Yeshua Wonders if He'd Consider Gilgamesh a Messiah," "Yeshua Rereads *Gilgamesh*. Ponders Shamhat, the Sex Worker," and "On His Way to a Wedding, Yeshua Stops in the Street" — These poems draw upon Stephen Langdon's exquisite translation of *Gilgamesh*. Italicized phrases in these poems, for instance, come from Mitchell's translation. Quotations are used with permission.

"Yeshua Borrows the *Iliad* from Rabbi's Library" — This poem, and the three poems following, draws from Robert Fagles's translation of the *Iliad* (Penguin Classics, 1998) by Homer. "And so the Trojans buried Hector breaker of horses" is a quotation from Fagles's translation. Excerpt from THE ILIAD by Homer, translated by Robert Fagles, translation copyright © 1990 by Robert Fagles. Used by permission of Viking Books, an imprint of Penguin Publishing Group, a division of Penguin Random House LLC. All rights reserved and used with permission.

"Yeshua Interviews Hebrew, Egyptian, Greek, and Mesopotamian Gods for His Research Project on Interfaith Dialogue" — This poem owes a debt to conversation with Helene Pasquin and Jay Albert and is dedicated to them.

"Yeshua Explains How Getting PrEP as a Young Adult Influenced His Ministry" — PrEP is a medication developed in the 2010s that, when used correctly, can help to prevent HIV infection.

"Hana Reminds Yeshua on Two Occasions that God Sends Angels to Spread His Heresy" — This poem is dedicated to Aryakorn Joy Phaphouvaninh.

"Yeshua Guesses Deuteronomy's Writer Had Never Been Kissed by a Man from Sodom," "Maybe Deuteronomy's Writer *Had* Been Kissed by a Man from Sodom," and "The Man from Sodom Explains Resurrection" — These poems dialogue with biblical descriptions of Sodom as a city known for sexual permissiveness.

"Yeshua Checks Out Fire Island" — Fire Island is a vacation destination on Long Island especially popular among the gay financially elite.

"Yeshua Heals a Gay Man" — The verse "I command you, come out of him and never enter him again" comes from Mark 9:25 (NIV).

"Mary Magdalene Sits Down for Coffee with a Fellow Writer at the Conference" — According to gnostic Christianity, Mary Magdalene is the scribe of the non-canonical "The Gospel of Mary." Here I imagine her responding to John 20:27 (NIV), in which Jesus convinces Thomas of his resurrection by offering Thomas his physical hand: "'Put your finger here,'" Jesus says; "'see my hands. Reach out your hand and put it into my side. Stop doubting and believe.'"

"Jesus Drafts His Paper for the Teachers Conference"— Italicized language belongs to Italian educator Maria Montessori, as quoted on the podcast "Great Lives" with host Matthew Parris and guest Philippa Perry, released on September 3, 2019.

"A Stoic and His Daughter Listen to the Apostle Paul": The phrase "the soul's first language" comes from Dr. Carl DuPont—artist, innovator, and educator—in conversation.

"The Podcast Host Asks Jesus to Explain Again Because Listeners Want to Understand" — The phrase "fear's gunk" comes from Mary Anne Burrows, brilliant teacher and spiritual mentor.

About the Author

Benjamin Bagocius, PhD, is associate professor of the humanities with Bard Early Colleges in Washington, D.C. He is founder and director of the Institute for Spiritual Poetry, which hosts writing workshops, group spiritual companioning, a journal, and other events. His poetry, essays, and academic articles also appear in a range of venues, including On Being, Tiferet, Pensive, Modernism/modernity, and is forthcoming in Studies in the Novel. Reach out and learn more at InstituteForSpiritualPoetry.com and BenjaminBagocius.com.

About Unsolicited Press

Unsolicited Press is based out of Portland, Oregon and focuses on the works of the unsung and underrepresented. As a womxn-owned, all-volunteer small publisher that doesn't worry about profits as much as championing exceptional literature, we have the privilege of partnering with authors skirting the fringes of the lit world. We've worked with emerging and award-winning authors such as Shann Ray, Amy Shimshon-Santo, Brook Bhagat, Kris Amos, and John W. Bateman.

Learn more at unsolicitedpress.com. Find us on twitter and instagram.

www.ingramcontent.com/pod-product-compliance
Lightning Source LLC
Chambersburg PA
CBHW031530120626
46545CB00005B/2089